About the Author

Hi there, I have been writing poetry since I was a young girl but more so since my poem *Queen* went viral. I feel empathy and I write as I feel. It is like I go deep within myself, and the words just flow from my heart. Writing is my true passion in life. I mostly write from another perspective to show there are always two sides to look from. I often move from my usual chair at home and sit in another and everywhere looks different. I am a simple lady with a lot of empathy.

Me, You and Mental Health, Too

Joanne Boyle

───────────────────────────────────────

Me, You and Mental Health, Too

Vanguard Press

VANGUARD PAPERBACK

© Copyright 2024
Joanne Boyle

The right of Joanne Boyle to be identified as author of this work has been asserted by them in accordance with the Copyright, Designs and Patents Act 1988.

All Rights Reserved

No reproduction, copy or transmission of this publication may be made without written permission.
No paragraph of this publication may be reproduced, copied or transmitted save with the written permission of the publisher, or in accordance with the provisions of the Copyright Act 1956 (as amended).

Any person who commits any unauthorised act in relation to this publication may be liable to criminal prosecution and civil claims for damages.

A CIP catalogue record for this title is available from the British Library.

ISBN 978 1 83794 115 5

Vanguard Press is an imprint of
Pegasus Elliot Mackenzie Publishers Ltd.
www.pegasuspublishers.com

First Published in 2024

Vanguard Press
Sheraton House Castle Park
Cambridge England

Printed & Bound in Great Britain

I dedicate this book to every single person, both young and old, who suffers with mental health problems. Just know someone cares. Reach out and let them in. Much love. Joanne xxx

Without all of you who read and resonate with my poems then I would not be writing them. Knowing I help others, also helps me. Thank you so much to all my friends on social media simply for caring and to my friends and family for loving me. xxx

Contents

You Me and Anxiety	13
I Am Nothing	14
The Butterfly	17
Another You!	21
The Invisible Illness	22
Warmth	23
I Am Sinking	25
Preloved	27
I smiled at you today	28
Nobody cares	29
Lost	32
The Security Blanket	33
Cheap Perfume	35
The Gossip and the Fly	37
Mental Health Awareness	38
Mental Health Awareness continued	39
The Porridge Bowl	41
Dementia Through the Keyhole	43
Under the Umbrella	44
The Undiagnosed	45
Post Natal Depression	49
The Friend	51
Addiction	52
Addiction and Its Family	53
Be the Light	54

You Me and Anxiety

You look at me and what do you see?
Someone worthless staring back at me.
You ask the mirror the questions.
Why, why don't you fit in?
Why do you bother to try?

You look at me and what do you see?
A big fat mess staring back at me.
You pull at your clothes to baggy them out,
Whilst inside your head you scream and shout.

You look at me and what do you see?
A lonely soul who just wants to be free.
You want to hide so no one will know,
The secret you carry and the places you go.

You look at me and what do you see?
A boy or a girl, he or she?
You are so confused in this head of yours,
You fear the outside and hate locked doors.

You look at me and what do you see?
A whole lot of anxiety staring back at me.
Look it in the eye for a minute or two,
And remind yourself it's not better than you.

I Am Nothing

I have eyes that see you there, yet I can't see you at all.
I have ears that hear noise, but they never hear your call.
I am nowhere to be found yet I am everywhere.
I am nothing but a shell, yet someone once lived there.

I have legs that walked for miles, but now they are still.
Arms I hug myself with in the hope that no one else will.
A numbness in my stomach, consumes my whole inside.
I don't care if I am seen as I have no energy to hide.

Love once lived in my heart, before I told it to move out.
I packed hope in my suitcase, along with any doubt.
In my mind there is a knocking, I hear it from within.
Then the silence follows, when it knows no one is in.

I am nothing but a shell since depression planted seeds.
I care nothing for the future, I no longer have any needs.
You feed me with pills, inject love into each one.
reminding me of times that to me are long gone.

One day I felt a flicker, a movement from my eye.
I saw a familiar face and I felt that I must try.
This 'nothing' I was feeling was now ready for a fight.
I was once again a somebody, who deserved this right.

The Butterfly

One day there was a caterpillar, it felt lost and so alone.
When it saw the other caterpillars, it would hide behind a stone.
For some reason this pretty caterpillar felt it didn't belong.
No matter how many times it was told that what it thought was wrong.
It was afraid it would be taunted, like it had been once before.
So, in its world of fantasy it would go off to explore.
Then this pretty caterpillar, heard a voice from nearby.
It opened its eyes and saw another caterpillar cry.
It asked it why it cried, as it wiped tears from its face.
The caterpillar answered how it always felt out of place.
From one caterpillar to another, it just couldn't understand.
"But you are so vibrant, you are what God had planned."
The caterpillar then stopped crying, but as they went to hug,
It realised it was its own reflection and it felt its heartstrings tug.
It then went on to open its own mind and saw a brighter world.
It looked for the nearest twig and off it went and curled.
It then transformed into a butterfly, so beautiful and free,
It then returned to the mirror and thought, 'Just look at me.'

It had spent so long believing in something that was not true,
When we all just need reminding that beauty is inside of you.

Another You!

Grief is but a simple word that carries so much meaning.
It has no specific definition and can make us feel demeaning.
Grief is born from loss, but loss can still be seen.
It does not only represent a someone who has once been.

It could be someone you know, where circumstance did change,
An illness could have stolen them, or an addiction made them strange.
The person could be yourself. Each day you are someone new.

With all kinds of grief, we just have to make it through.
Grief has so many branches, but leaves don't ever grow.
They just keep reaching out with their nakedness on show.
Grief is surrounded by colour, but it remains black and white.
It represents an emptiness that is lost from others' sight.
Grief shall always win each battle in your mind,
So, we meet 'Another You' at each obstacle that we find.

The Invisible Illness

I don't know who you are. I cannot see your face.
How dare you come along, invading my head space?

How dare you punch my thoughts, fists curled up tight?
How dare you run a marathon as I try to sleep at night?

In my defence I try to fight, but with whom I don't know.
You are nothing but a coward, yet still I feel low.

You are everywhere I am. Just leave me alone.
Kicking at my conscience and picking every bone.

You are on every corner, in every room that I enter.
Everyone is judging me but it's you in the centre.

No one hears me scream or shout for you to go.
You continue with your gnawing, waiting for me to blow.

I grabbed on to myself in the hope that I was seen.
Sure, enough I was, at last somewhere for me to lean.

Someone out there cared. Heard me instead of you, and
not only did you crumble… You ran from my head, too.

Warmth

I woke up this morning feeling rather blue.
I pulled the blankets closer and pretended they were you.
I felt them wrap around me and closed my eyes again.
I went back to a time I never felt this pain.

I put my head into the pillow. I inhaled your scent,
I tried to bring you back from wherever it was you went.
The blankets kept me warm, like the tears on my cheeks.
Not sure how long it's been, if it's been days or weeks.

I went into a dream in the hope you'd find me there.
To a time when togetherness was what we loved to share.
When smiling was normal and laughter born from fun,
Back to the beginning of where our journey had begun.

The warmth now engulfs me. I can feel you here.
I am wrapped in your arms as you wipe away my tear.
Don't try to wake me up. Leave me in this place.
Stop giving me that look when I look up at your face.

I don't want to hear you saying, my life must go on,
or that I should be grateful that I still have one.
I open my eyes just then as I know that you are right.
I shall find my way of coping and won't give up my fight.

I Am Sinking

Throw me a rope, I am sinking. I really don't want to drown.
I am just sick of gurgling water. I am tired of feeling down.
I miss a life I had, all the things I've lost.
I am tired of paying the price, regardless of the cost.

I am the captain of this ship and my responsibilities include
sailing through stormy waters and brightening up your mood.
My name is Captain Faith, my ship goes by the name of *Hope*.
I shall get you to the shore, keep a hold on to that rope.

The rope is starting to fray. The water is above my head.
I see my family weeping as I recall the things they said.
Pass me some tape to bind this, so I can last a little longer,
anything at all, to make it a little stronger.

As captain of this ship, my priority is my crew.
My arms will replace the rope that you are holding on to.
I will steer the wheel until we make it to the shore.
Then, my dear friend, you won't need that rope any more.

Preloved

Discarded like old clothing,
that didn't fit you any more.
Thrown upon a heap,
on a dirty bedroom floor.

I was your favourite shirt
Worn with your best suit.
You wore me on your arm.
I shone like a polished boot.

We danced around the moon
Sat under the red-hot sun.
We laughed at the same things.
Together was just fun.

Then off fun went running,
to someone else's arms.
The jokes we had shared,
now someone else's charms.

This heap that I now sat upon,
with tears down my face,
had a sign above the door,
saying this is Prelove's Place.

I smiled at you today

I smiled at you today, though I never knew your name.
You never smiled back, that was such a shame.
Now I go on walking, asking what I do wrong.
This is just the beginning of thinking I don't belong.

I now bow my head. The smile gone from my face.
It's now replaced with dread on my journey to my place.
Is it the way I look? Or because of the clothes I wear?
I wish I could switch off. I wish I did not care.

Maybe I should have asked if it was something I'd done.
Just thinking of the asking makes me want to run.
I know I must fight this. This war is in my head.
These people aren't my enemies who fill me with dread.

They know not what they do, so it must be I?
I wish I had the answers, to all my questions why?
The day has just begun but is decided by your smile.
Would it have really hurt to make my day worthwhile?

I stopped off at the shop, to get myself a drink.
I then took a minute, to process the way I think.
The shop assistant chatted. I was invisible to her eye.
It was time to stand my ground, so I shouted, *"This is I!"*

Nobody cares

When you think nobody cares, how broken you are,
or you think they can't understand.
When even the outside feels too small,
and you no longer want a hand.
When the sky feels like it's suffocating,
and the ground is hurting your feet,
When the smile becomes a fake hello
to the people that you greet,
When the reasons don't matter
and there is nothing left to give,
When the empty hole becomes
the place you want to live.
When everyone around you
becomes invisible to your eye,
When you are drained of all emotion,
with no tears left to cry.
When love can no longer save you,
and you are in the depths despair.
You have gone deaf to all the voices,
that scream, "Hang in there!"

Yet the world is still uneducated and
none know what to do,
because if listening was enough,
then it would have saved you.

Lost

I haven't seen you for a while,
I wondered where you went.
I walked down every avenue
but I couldn't find your scent.

I shouted out your name,
in the hope that you would hear.
I walked down familiar paths,
to see if you were near.

I looked at all your clothes,
put some on like you once did.
They didn't feel the same.
I wondered where you'd hid.

I went into your home,
I walked into your room.
I took one look in the mirror,
and saw the darkness loom.

Depression is a disguise,
like an old jumper that you wear.
I will never give up looking for you,
as I know you're still in there.

The Security Blanket

You woke me up this morning just so you could see,
the person beneath the eyes wasn't really me.
You made me look outside, even though I was so weak.
You said there was tomorrow. You said the same all week.
You pushed me back to bed; said you'd take care of it all.
You told me if I slept, it would save me from a fall.
You told me not to eat, that in time I would be thin.
You understood my mind, you heard me from within.
You spoke about tomorrow, all the things that we would do.
I knew it was a lie, but I tried to believe in you.
You said you'd mind the kids, that you'd watch them play.
You said they didn't need me; they were better off this way.
I thought you were my friend, so I gave you all my trust.
Admittedly, I gave it easily as I saw it as a must.
Then I heard you talking. You were whispering my name.
I heard you say I'd given up and my life was not the same.
Those words pricked my mind, though the prick was small.
I got out of bed that morning and pushed against the wall.
I looked outside the window, but I saw something new.
I saw a glimmer of hope, I pictured a different view.

I called upon a person, I did not care just who,
I knew I was worth fighting for and that I'd make it through.
I would go on searching for who I used to be because somewhere inside I knew there was still a Me.

Cheap Perfume

So, you bought me for a nickel?
To put me on a shelf.
Only took me out,
to ease your mental health.
You'd dab me here and there,
depending on the place,
to try to make an impression,
and only show one face.

When I was of no use,
I would be left for days,
other perfumes being favoured,
by your disrespectful ways.
One day when I wasn't needed,
and I had lost my smell,
you didn't even care enough,
to ask if I was well.

When you only spend a nickel,
then expect something cheap.
A true friend deserves better,
so, sow what you reap.
An investment will bring quality,
for a priceless treasure,
and if it's taken care of,
you'll have a friend forever.

The Gossip and the Fly

When I had no one to talk to as no one else was there,
I had something on my mind, I felt the need to share.

So, I spoke about my thoughts, just momentary words,
not thinking for a moment, how they would be shared.

Neither did I care as the truth it has no lies,
but the truth becomes lost by the mouths of flies.

They land upon a wall, listen to all that is said,
then go to another room to twist things in their head.

They go buzzing all around, adding to their news.
What amazes me most is how others have their views.

Playing Chinese Whispers, not caring who is hurt.
All that matters to them is the gossip that they spurt.

The fly doesn't realise that it isn't worth very much,
yet it causes so much damage in all that it does touch.

One day they found the truth that hid beneath the lie.
A person had been damaged through a gossip and a fly.

Mental Health Awareness

I sat and played with the demons in my head,
setting my pulse on fire, as my body filled with dread.

Looking out of the window, why is it always so dark?
Praying for some silence from every sound and bark.

I feel the sweat falling from my brow,
caused simply by my thoughts as I question, 'How?'

How do I escape? To run from my own mind.
To dig for an answer, knowing there's none to find.

To sit upon this chair that ties me up in chains,
knowing no one cares and nothing else remains.

To hope and pray for an answer, for someone just to see.
Beneath this mask I wear, will someone look at me?

But still, I do not tell. I let my demons win.
No one really cares enough, so why should I let them in?

Instead, I'll sit and rot, the stench consuming my soul.
I will lock my door and climb inside that deep dark hole.

The world outside will listen then to all words unsaid.
Then they will really care, so it's better if I am dead.

Mental Health Awareness continued

We cared for you, my friend; we simply didn't know.
We only saw you smiling. We saw what you did show.

We are sorry you never noticed, when the sun did shine,
Or found serenity from the music as you drank red wine.

We are sorry for those chains. Wished we'd had the key.
We did not read your eyes as they begged for us to see.

We are sorry for your family. For all who hurt today.
We are sorry you didn't trust anyone, to be able to stay.

We are sorry for your pain. We all now pay the price.
We only wish you had seen that people can be nice.

So now we live and learn, from one battle that is lost.
That we will build an army due to the lives it's cost.

My message to all of you, is don't listen with your ears.
Our eyes are more perceptive to see a person's fears.

The Porridge Bowl

Eating a bowl of porridge, I haven't brushed my hair,
drowning in each spoonful, willing myself to care.
A little bit missed my mouth, I wiped it with my sleeve.
Is this the life I've chosen; born from a life I grieve?

I go back to the chair. It's still warm from where I sat.
I look at the familiar surroundings, yet I wonder where I'm at.
I can feel myself sinking to the bottom of my bowl.
Knowing every bit I swallow, isn't enough to fill this hole.

My bowl is now empty, and I look toward the sink.
I drag myself from the chair, but I'm finding it hard to think.
I know I must keep moving. To remind myself of worth.
I look outside the window and see the beauty of the Earth.

I decide to turn the tap though I felt a wrench was needed,
I just tried a little harder as I had once proceeded.
When the tap was turned and I saw the water run,
the dripping of my happy times had once again begun.

I took myself to the shower. A task within itself.
I took my favourite soap from the dusty shelf.
As I began to scrub, I felt my troubles wash away.
I was proud of what I'd done and could now face the day.

Dementia Through the Keyhole

It's like looking through a keyhole at someone you don't
    know.
Forgetting who you are or where you want to go.
Seeing only segments of who you used to be.
Not able to distinguish which one is really me.

In one moment, you have a family, the next you are a child,
living with broken pieces from a life once compiled.
Not knowing who is there or even where you are,
yet knowing you are somewhere, feeling so bizarre.

Every minute spent forgetting the moment that has passed.
Every day a new beginning because you forgot the last.
Piecing together a jigsaw of every moment every day,
without realising that a vital piece was thrown away.

Looking in the mirror and wondering who it is you see.
Sitting at the table wondering who is sitting with me.
Asking for your parents who passed so long ago, and
wondering where your kids are as you forgot you saw them
    grow.

Looking through the keyhole at a life that you've forgot,
but loved ones will remember to make sure that it's not.
They will hold the key that will unlock the door,
to a lifetime full of memories, you don't have any more.

Under the Umbrella

Sometimes things overwhelm me, and I don't know what to do,
I just want to be alone and to be away from you.
It doesn't mean that I don't love you, or that I don't care,
It just means I am frustrated, and I don't know how to share.

My emotions have run through me like a fast train on a track,
I am not sure how to react, but I'll find my own way back.
So, leave me on my own and give me some space!
Stop it with your words, please move out of my face.

Holding The Umbrella

I will be right behind you no matter where you go.
I promise to keep my distance and my silence, so you know.
You see you are my family and no matter what you do.
I will try to understand what you are going through.

I will always love you and that means every little part.
Blood has made us family, but we are connected at the heart.
So, no matter what you need or how much you run away,
I am not going anywhere; I am here to stay.

The Undiagnosed

I made my way to work today and at times that's hard to do.
I worry about the people and if I will make it through.
I looked inside the file where the rotas are kept.
I saw it had been changed and felt the disrespect.

My heart began to race. I don't take to change.
I felt I couldn't cope and how I was seen as strange.
I did not know who to speak to as my voice locked up inside.
I do not like confrontation. I would rather run and hide.

Then you spoke down to me. I knew other people heard.
I didn't understand but I know that I felt scared.
If I was a child, would you have had more respect?
Or speak to me the same, with intellectual neglect?

I had to say good morning, but I wanted to get away.
People may think I am ignorant, but I just don't know what to say.
I love being on my own, yet I speak all day long,
about how I wish you would understand all that you do wrong.

Children are diagnosed and understood so much more,

but what about the adults who come walking through the door?
Don't their feelings matter because now they are all grown?
They may be 'Undiagnosed', but awareness should be shown.

Post Natal Depression

You see a mother with a baby. You stop to take a peek.
Inside my head I'm screaming, it's the same every week.

You see a smiling face. You don't see behind the eyes.
You think it's only natural when my baby cries.

I think of other mummies who make it look so easy.
Standing looking beautiful, take to it all so naturally.

I am a prisoner who's lost inside her thoughts.
Wondering what is wrong? Why do I feel so distraught?

Thinking I'm not good enough, my baby deserves much more.
Questioning my own movements, asking what it's all for.

Praying for my bedtime to find it is then day.
Locked inside a dwelling, not knowing what to say.

Overwhelmed by uncertainty, by what others might think,
just wanting to escape yet too scared to even blink.

Feeling like an inmate in the eyes of others.
Feeling like a culprit in front of the other mothers.

Depression is an illness unseen by those around but
help is always there since mental health was found.

The Friend

We sat upon the bench. We shared a currant bun.
We didn't need words or have anywhere to run.
We sat in silence as the wind whistled in our ears.
I looked to my right and saw you shed a tear.

I let that tear fall. It was all that I could do.
You knew you had a friend, sitting right beside you.
Nothing else was needed at this moment and this time,
just having someone there in a moment of sublimity.

I could see your chest moving, now the tears fell hard.
Still, I ate my currant bun, I wasn't playing any card.
I knew when you were ready, it didn't matter when.
I would still be sitting beside you. There was never a 'now
 and then'.

I don't know why you cried or how you felt inside.
I was just glad that I was sitting there by your side.
Then you looked at me and I saw it written on your face,
thankful to have a friend sharing your darkest place.

Addiction

I hate who I have become, you wouldn't understand.
I once had hopes and dreams, this isn't what I planned.

I just felt so insecure, and I heard it call out to me,
"Come and give it a go and I will set your spirits free."

I thought I'd try it once, not giving tomorrow a thought,
I cared about the moment and the confidence I sought.

I didn't think that it would harm, I didn't think at all,
How could a little powder cause someone to fall?

I really loved that feeling and my body just craved more,
It became a battle of will and I lost track of what it was for.

So, then the lying started and so did hating me,
I turned to my new friend who was also my enemy.

I hurt the ones I love and myself along the way.
The only way to forget was to take it every day.

Inside I cry out loud for you to remember that I am inside,
This broken addict you see, was just a place to hide.

Addiction and Its Family

I hung around with you today even though I knew I shouldn't.
Mum said that you would knock but I said you wouldn't.

I tried to keep you a secret, but mums always know.
They can read us inside out, pointless putting on a show.

I should have told you to go. Instead, I broke her heart.
You knew this would happen right from the very start.

I thought I was invincible and stronger than the others,
after all they were only stories made up by other mothers.

At least we had some fun times that only we can share.
at the time that's all that matters, not those who truly care.

When I have no money and you are nowhere to be found,
I find myself alone, sleeping on the ground.

It's then I miss you most, not my parents or my friends.
It's then I do more damage in the hope the feeling ends.

I wish I had listened to my mum; not let you call on me.
I was once a happy soul from a loving family.

I should have asked your name, but you have many
for the ones they use, the difference isn't any.
Drugs!

Be the Light

Be the light to someone's dark,
the day to someone's night.
Be the anchor to their rope,
the flame to their ignite.
Be the answer to their question,
the ears to their sorrow.
Be their voice of silence,
their reason for tomorrow.
Be the umbrella to their rain,
the roof to keep them dry.
Be the hand that wipes the tears,
every time they cry.
Be the dance they want to learn,
the song they want to sing.
Be the friend they need,
be their everything.
Be the cushion on the sofa,
the rug upon the floor.
Be the home they need,
when they come through the front door.